ROUGH

Warships Fight

by

Mike Critchley & Steve Bush

CW00382603

HMS ARK ROYAL pushes on through an Indian Ocean whipped by Hurricane Ivy in March 1966. (Mike Critchley Collection)

Roughers Rough seas: "I enjoy a spot of roughers - no queues in the galley for a fried breakfast.." (As defined in *Jackspeak*)

This book is published as a result of many superb photographs arriving on the desk of our magazine ***WARSHIP WORLD*** thanks to our readers. A few have been published within that magazine but we thought this collection of photos sent in from around the world worthy of a wider audience. The number to hand (in 2001) has become enough to fill this volume - and possibly another if the flow of new material continues to arrive here. Do you have material that could be of interest to us?

We are indebted to all those who contributed to this book, but particularly to ex-RFA Officers George Mortimore and Stuart Talton who had their cameras to hand in some of the foulest weather imaginable during their seagoing careers.

It is often said by "Old Salts" that today's sailors don't know what rough weather is! From the photographs presented between these covers the reader may conclude otherwise. Before browsing further we suggest you have a good breakfast inside you - you may not feel like it before you get to the end of the book! Or can we recommend the shipping forecast on BBC Radio 4 at midnight once you are tucked up in bed?

Mike Critchley & Steve Bush

Liskeard
Cornwall

November 2001

The battleship BENBOW pushing hard into a gale in the Bay of Biscay in the mid 1930's demonstrating the seas total contempt for these man made leviathans.
(Tim Chevasse)

Taking it green - Whilst the seas appear not to be whipped up by the wind there is clearly a big swell running as this Squadron of "R" class battleships try to maintain station.
(Steve Bush Collection)

This series of photographs was taken in the mid 1930's. (Steve Bush Collection)

"A ship in harbour is safe. But that is not what ships are built for." (John Shedd). The battleship RESOLUTION proving the point as she comes up for a breath of air whilst on Home Fleet Exercises in 1934. (Ben Warlow Collection)

The cruiser DIOMEDE ploughing through rough seas during three weeks of Northern Patrol duties during the winter months of 1939. The windscreen of the open bridge offered little protection to the bridge crew from the tons of spray heading their way! The simple expedient of putting a roof on the bridge would improve the lot of the watchkeepers a thousand fold. It is easy to forget however, that at this time the ship was fought and maneouvered from the bridge. Without radar, particularly whilst under air attack, it was down to the Mk 1 eyeball to keep the enemy in sight and position the ship accordingly. Difficult to do if you have a roof over your head! (Bert Channon)

Patrolling north of Iceland the battlecruiser RENOWN noses in to the North Atlantic pushing aside tons of sea water. Note the turret is trained aft over the starboard side.
(Jean Coultas)

Not only did rough seas pound both men and machinery but in the northern latitudes the constant freezing spray created problems with icing. Here the RENOWN takes on a very wintry look as snow and ice cover her decks and guardrails. It was a constant battle between men (with their axes and steam hoses) and the elements to keep the ice under control as it dramatically increased topweight and compromised stability. (Jean Coultas)

Duffle coats, oilskins and sweaters
Are the matelots daily rig,
Clinging close to precious lifelines
Moaning, howling, life's a jig.
Guns that burn through frostbitten fingers
Ere the shot has been rammed home,
Steady there, then how she quivers,
Shells are spewed across the foam.

Cables creaking, hawsers screeching,
Wind and tempest 'gainst man's pride,
Grim the waters, white capped cauldrons
Smash and buffet 'gainst ship's side.
Now she shudders, now she's steady,
Firm hands grasp the heavy wheel,
Ice-rimmed eyes, bright in red sockets,
Hold her on an even keel.
(H. Binton)

The bridge crew keep watch from their lofty perch as CUMBERLAND patrols the northern wastes in the early 1940's. (Jim Harrison)

The carrier COURAGEOUS demonstrating the disadvantages of a lower flying off deck. Even in moderate seas, once at speed the bows are soon awash.
(Fleet Air Arm Museum)

A fine action shot taken in 1942 of DUKE OF YORK whilst firing a broadside. This picture illustrates well the reputation that these battleships had for being wet forward. Although the sea is not that rough, the sea is breaking over the decks in the region of "A" turret. (D.G. Matthews)

Midnight in the Arctic Circle in 1943. Another King George V class battleship, this time ANSON almost disappears from sight as she steams at speed into a heavy swell. A combination of high speed and heavy swell can make for some very interesting mealtimes below decks! (George Huddart Collection)

It is February 1943 and the bridge crew of SHEFFIELD have a grandstand view of one of the worst storms to hit the North Atlantic. Unable to make headway in the mountainous seas she hove to (keeping the propellors going to provide sufficient headway) to keep her bows pointed into the sea. As the accompanying barograph shows the pressure fell rapidly with the ship facing 150 mph winds and rising seas..... (Charles Addis Collection)

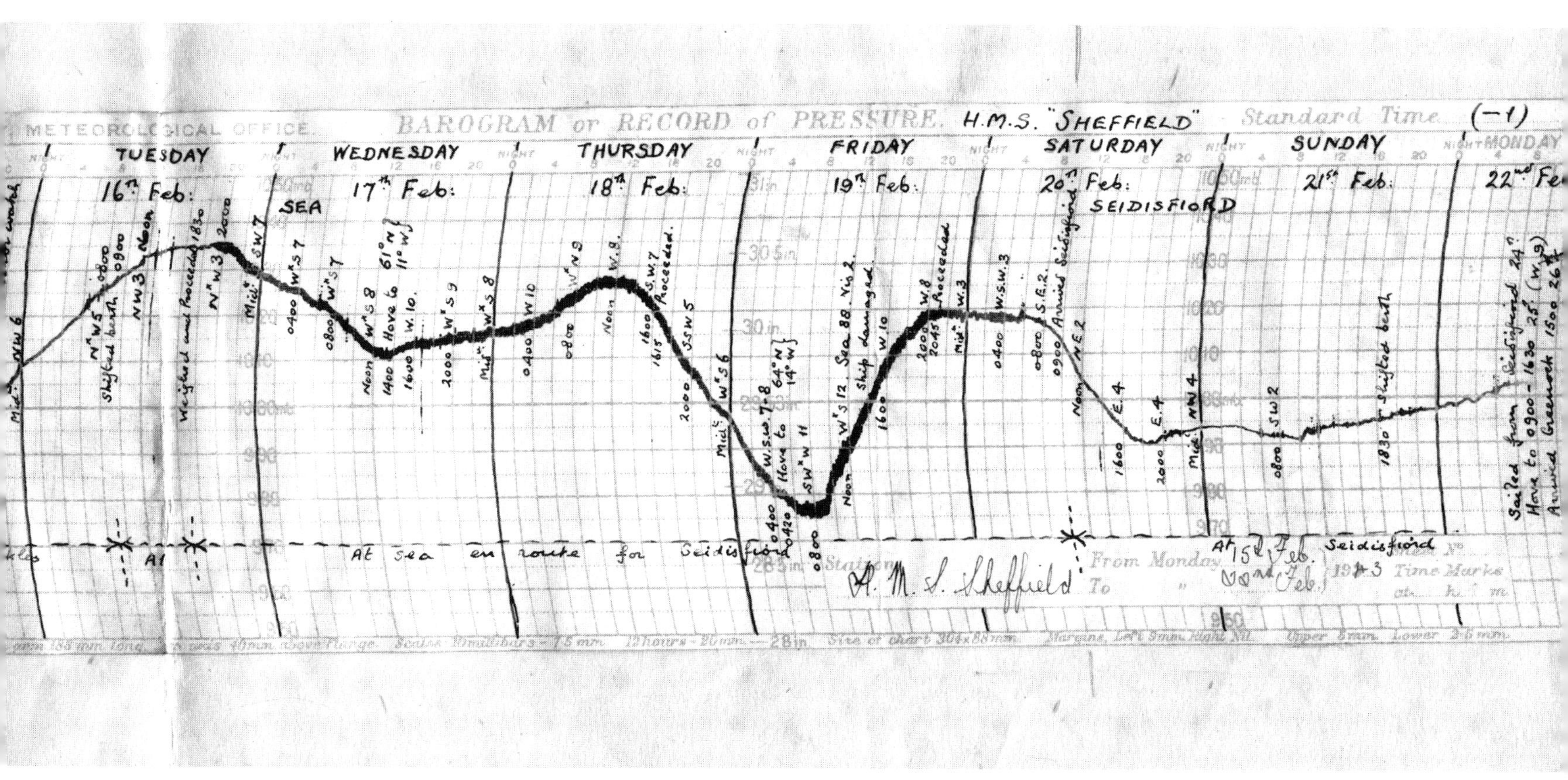

The SHEFFIELD's barograph for the period clearly shows the dramatic drop in pressure over 18/19 February. (Charles Addis Collection)

.......As the mountainous seas crashed down on the ship they partially ripped away the roof of "A" turret allowing hundreds of tons of seawater to enter the ship. SHEFFIELD endured the storm for 12 hours before it began to blow itself out. All forward decks were damaged, "A" turret was totally bent and jammed and the ship had been blown 200 miles off course. An object lesson in the immense power of the sea.

(Charles Addis Collection)

In rough weather life on board the smaller vessels degenerated into an endless misery of violent motion, lack of sleep and cold wet clothes. The sweep deck of this Algerine class minesweeper is awash. Visible are the paravanes and otters, securely stowed. Anything not properly lashed down in this weather would soon be lost to the sea.
(Eric Drummond)

Life onboard an Algerine! - In conditions like these men had not only to fight the U-Boats and mines, but the elements as well. The upperdeck would in peacetime be out of bounds in such conditions since it was near impossible to retain ones footing. But in times of war, upperdeck weapons and guns, usually in open turrets, had to be manned despite being exposed to the full force of the weather. (Eric Drummond)

The small Escort Carriers with their high freeboard suffered in heavy seas. Here, EMPEROR pitches into yet another wall of water whilst trying to maintain station. Another vessel is just visible through the gloom on the horizon. (Ben Warlow Collection)

Eternal Father, strong to save,
Whose arm doth bind the restless wave,
Who bid'st the mighty ocean deep
Its own appointed limits keep;
O hear us when we cry to thee
For those in peril on the sea.

This picture clearly illustrates the differing forces at work on a ships hull in these conditions. The ships pitching motion (forward to aft) is combined with a rolling motion (port to starboard) making the ship appear to corkscrew through the sea. This is usually accompanied by the sound of breaking crockery and curses from within the ship itself! Flying aircraft on or off in these conditions is impossible. If the chains securing the aircraft to the deck were removed the planes would simply slide off the deck into the sea. (Ben Warlow Collection)

The Battle class destroyer CADIZ about to start a jackstay transfer during the winter of 1949/50. (John Carder)

The Australian River class frigate MACQUARIE crashing through a swell in the Great Australian Bight in 1952. Life in these small vessels could be quite lonely in rough weather. As you speed into a trough the world around you becomes a wall of sea, then once you are shot up to the top of the next crest you momentarily see the ships around you before plunging out of sight once again into the next trough. (Royal Australian Navy)

The destroyer DELIGHT photographed in the English Channel in the 1950's. (W. H. Hatto Collection)

You know it's rough when a huge aircraft carrier disappears from view! In September 1953 INDEFATIGABLE lifts her skirts and ploughs into yet another trough whilst on a training cruise with her sister IMPLACABLE off the Scilly Isles. This sort of sea, lifting the stern clear of the water puts tremendous strain on both the shafts and the "A" brackets as the propellors, released from the drag of the water, thrash wildly in the air. (A.J. Stait)

"They that go down to the sea in ships, that do business in great waters: These see the works of the Lord and his wonders in the deep" (Psalm 107 : 23). Here WAVE VICTOR, an appropriate name, trails a hose over her stern as she prepares to fuel a battleship in a "marginal sea state." (MoD/Crown Copyright)

"Woe to you, O destroyer....." (Isaiah 33:1). The Weapon class destroyer SCORPION lifts her nose out of the water while operating in heavy weather in Northern waters during Exercise Mariner 1953. (G. Davies Collection)

“See, I will stir up the spirit of a destroyer....” (Jeremiah 51:1). The Australian Destroyer TOBRUK emerges from a deep trough in the Southern Ocean.
(Royal Australian Navy)

The Type 15 frigate URSA operating in the "balmy blue" Mediterranean in 1958.... (Ton Class Association)

Although not of the best quality, these pictures had to be included. "Are you a ship or a submarine?" That was the signal sent to the inshore minesweeper BASSINGHAM captured here disappearing behind yet another wave by a photographer on FORT SANDUSKY. The tiny BASSINGHAM was being delivered to the East African Navy in September 1958 when caught by the tail end of two cyclones whilst on passage (off the South African coast) to Mombasa, Kenya.

(Cdr P.J. Clarke RN (The CO of BASSINGHAM))

The frigate LYNX was serving on the South Africa Station when pictured off Madagascar in 1959. The picture was taken in the Mozambique Channel from the stern bofors gallery of ALBION on passage to Durban . Behind schedule and trying to make Durban at the appointed time LYNX was advised to tuck in under ALBION's quarter to take advantage of what "shelter" there was. It is not recorded whether she made it in one piece, or indeed why the sonar dome was in the lowered position in this weather.

(Ben Newton)

Rough seas make for dramatic pictures but it is likely that in such conditions many of the crew will part company with the contents of their stomachs. The New Zealand minesweeper INVERELL tests the stamina of her crew as it pounds through the Tasman Sea in the 1960's. (Vic Jeffrey Collection)

Although better suited to cope with surface transits than modern submarines with their teardrop hull forms, the American submarine SENNET still ships water even in a moderate sea. (Ben Newton)

"....for suddenly the destroyer will come upon us" (Jeremiah 6:26). Photographed in May 1962 BROADSWORD is shown at speed and with all guns firing.
(Imperial War Museum Neg MH 27487)

Another washing down for the upper deck as the frigate ASHANTI punches into the swell in July 1964. (MoD/Crown Copyright)

“Wouldst thou' - so the helmsman answered -
'Learn the secret of the sea?
Only those who brave its dangers
Comprehend its mystery.”

Were these words of Longfellow ringing in the ears of her crew as the South African minesweeper DURBAN negotiated the narrow Knysna passage to escape the stormy conditions off the coast?

(Allan du Toit Collection)

March 1966 saw ARK ROYAL heading for the Mozambique Channel to instigate a Beira patrol. Hurricane Ivy was also in the area! (Mike Critchley Collection)

The frigate ULYSSES digs her bows into an apparently calm sea. Even without being whipped up by the wind a long low swell can provide dramatic moments for a speeding ship.
(Dave Scoble Collection)

The small single screw Type 14 frigate RUSSELL demonstrates her seakeeping qualities whilst operating on a Joint Maritime Course in 1966. The picture was submitted by a young inexperienced signalman. He left the ship very experienced - and cured of his seasickness! (Richard Price Collection)

In September 1970 CAVALIER intercepted an SOS during night exercises in a heavy storm in the Bristol Channel. A coaster was on fire and had been abandoned, apparently about to sink. However, the ship stayed afloat and after standing by for 36 hours in heavy weather and with the wreck nearing the coast, the CAVALIER succeeded in putting a boarding party onboard and passing a tow. Despite the tow parting the destroyer reached Milford Haven with the coaster in tow 52 hours after the original SOS! (MoD/Crown Copyright)

A harbour is not always a guarantee of protection from rough weather! This pair of S Class submarines are seen alongside the depot ship MAIDSTONE - inside Portland harbour! When the wind used to blow, it was just like being at sea, indeed when it got really bad and the boats started bumping together, it was a regular occurrence to cast off and head for the safety of the sea. (Alfie Roake)

The Type 12 frigate RHYL in 1967... **"Once a ship starts to move in a seaway, objects which are not secured are liable to fall out of their stowage and may break and cause damage to personnel and ship's fittings"** ***Naval Ratings' Handbook*, *1938*.** (Ben Warlow Collection)

Living up to her name the frigate RELENTLESS, experiencing the relentless pounding of the sea! (Dave Scoble Collection)

The Australian Daring class destroyer VAMPIRE pounds through the Southern Ocean in 1969. She is now preserved and open to the public in the usually calmer waters of Sydney Harbour.
(Royal Australian Navy)

An unknown destroyer, thought to be CONTEST. "....So the Officer of the Watch said to me he had a foolproof cure for seasickness. "Whats that?" I said. "Find a large Oak tree....and sit under it." he replied - whilst clinging to the side of the Bridge. (Mike Critchley Collection)

A quick snap from the bridge of the guided missile destroyer DEVONSHIRE as she too is caught out in the wrong ocean on the wrong day! And people still want to cross the Atlantic in rowing boats and tiny sailing craft! (Peter Harrison)

Big ship...even bigger sea. The Commando carrier BULWARK caught out in a Hurricane in the North Atlantic - 16th January 1974. (Ben Warlow Collection)

The carrier ARK ROYAL sends her aircraft through the car wash......It is unclear if the Gannet aircraft (top left) has just taken off or is looking for somewhere more appropriate to land. (Lt Cdr Peter Cunningham Collection)

Strong Gale - High waves, dense streaks of foam, crests start to topple, tumble, roll over; spray may affect visibility. (Beaufort Wind Scale definition). Although conditions for ARETHUSA appear dramatic, they are far short of a strong gale. (Jim Patchett Collection)

Not many people know that frigates have angled flight decks too. Here the photographer onboard the frigate SIRIUS takes the shot to prove the fact!! (Steve Bush)

Even aircraft carriers are not immune to rough weather. Here Sea Harriers of 800 Naval Air Squadron get a soaking from the sea whilst parked on the flight deck of HERMES. When the weather improved they would need a good fresh water wash to prevent the corrosive sea water getting to work. The depth of water flooding down the flight deck can be seen around the aircraft wheels. (MoD/Crown Copyright)

Better than a ride on the big dipper at the fun fair? Seamen on the frigate SIRIUS haul in the fuel hose from a tanker to enable them to take onboard much needed fuel. She is seen here patrolling the Iceland/Faroes gap on anti-submarine patrol on a bleak February day in 1985. (Stuart Talton)

Built as "coastal" minesweepers in the 1950's these Ton class vessels went on to serve in the four corners of the World -frequently far away from coastal waters. With a shallow draught and high freeboard these vessels were always known as "lively" seaboats. HUBBERSTON is seen here in 1988. (MoD/Crown Copyright)

Photographed during the Falklands War in 1982 BROADSWORD had to contend with the wild seas of the South Atlantic as well as the Argentine Air Force (the rust streaks on the hangar sides are holes from Argentine cannon fire). (MoD/Crown Copyright)

Another Falklands War photograph. Here the Type 21 frigate AVENGER shows off her underwater paintwork as she takes fuel onboard on the long haul back to the UK from the South Atlantic in 1982. (Mike Critchley Collection)

Yet more from the Falklands War. The deep sea trawler JUNELLA was commissioned as an HM ship and pressed into service as a minesweeper in the South Atlantic.
(Mike Critchley Collection)

Nothing like a bracing trip across Lyme Bay with the wind and spray in your face....The bridge watchkeepers of the fast training boat CUTLASS "enjoyed" an open bridge - in the summer! (MoD/Crown Copyright)

Even in the Gulf of Aden flat calm seas are not promised. Here the French frigate COMMANDANTE RIVIERE prepares to come alongside PLUMLEAF (in November 1982) for fuel.
(George Mortimore)

Just what the designers wanted. The low sleek bow of the frigate YARMOUTH cuts through the swell whilst on patrol in the West Indies in September 1984.
(George Mortimore)

The huge bulk of OLMEDA is hardly affected by the force of the sea as she ploughs into the South China Sea in 1984 (Stuart Talton)

A good day off the North Cape in April 1984...Frequently the weather is far worse than this! Here ACHILLES closes the RFA tanker GREY ROVER for fuel. The fuel hose is already turned out ready to be connected inboard (behind the gun turret) of the frigate. (George Mortimore)

Even 30,000 ton tankers are thrown around by the massive power of the sea. The replenishment tanker TIDESPRING has put her bow into a wave in the "roaring forties" and brought many hundred tons of salt water up whilst pitching in heavy weather. (M J Nurse)

Leander Class frigates (and the Type 12 frigates before them) were renowned for their excellent sea keeping characteristics. Their long foc'sle and thin hull gave them the ability to punch through seas that would slow other vessels down. It must be Friday.....as the frigate BACCHANTE is heading at speed for Liverpool for the weekend in June 1980. She is seen here travelling at over 20 knots in the Irish sea. (MoD/Crown Copyright)

A long North Atlantic swell sees ARGONAUT approaching GREY ROVER for fuel in September 1984. The seamen who will carry out the replenishment (the equipment is prepared just forward of the bridge) are out of sight below decks until the frigate is in position closer to the tanker. (George Mortimore)

Just a grey day in the North Atlantic. Grey ship, grey sky and a grey sea in November 1985 as the frigate PHOEBE comes alongside a tanker for fuel. The tanker is GREY ROVER - of course. (George Mortimore)

Another shower for anyone caught on the upper deck at the wrong time. The frigate BRILLIANT was crossing the Atlantic as part of the Standing Naval Force Atlantic in 1985 when photographed by Leading Airman Kevin Jeffries. (MoD/Crown Copyright)

The Type 21 frigates paid the price of being worked hard in rough weather. They needed strengthening down the ships side - amidships - to prevent further hull cracking Here ACTIVE is seen operating in the Portland exercise areas in 1986. (MoD/Crown Copyright)

The Type 42 destroyer MANCHESTER exercising off Hawaii in 1986. Not a good day to be preparing lunch in the galley. (MoD/Crown Copyright)

When a tanker and any other warship get in close company to refuel the sea tends to "boil" between them as the water pressure between them both has little room to escape Here OLMEDA is photographed from ILLUSTRIOUS off Tasmania during exercises in 1986. (David Fortey)

When it really gets rough the only way a warship can get its vital fuel supplies is for the tanker to stream a fuel hose astern and the receiving ship grapple to bring it inboard. Here the frigate PHOEBE takes fuel from BLUE ROVER in May 1989. The hose can just be seen in the foreground as the frigate is snapped "bow down" in the trough of a wave.
(George Mortimore)

A well known recruiting photo of MINERVA and her Lynx helicopter operating off Portland on a "typical Portland day" (MoD/Crown Copyright)

Even in the South China sea it's not always calm....Here the Hong Kong patrol boat PLOVER shows a clean pair of heels as she undertakes a patrol looking for illegal immigrants in local waters. (Mike Critchley Collection)

Photographed from GREY ROVER (Feb 1986) in the Western Approaches SOUTHAMPTON approaches the tanker to take on fuel. Note the gun turret turned through 180 degrees to prevent salt water damage around the barrel. (George Mortimore)

The Norwegian frigate NARVIK approaches GREY ROVER for fuel - also in February 1986. These tiny frigates are used to operating in much rougher weather off Northern Norway, long after photographers have packed their cameras away and retired to their bunks. (George Mortimore)

Not a particularly rough day but a tight turn at speed has plenty of spray flying about the place over the destroyer BIRMINGHAM. (MoD/Crown Copyright)

Off the Australian coast a long swell can have vessels jumping about the place as this picture of the Australian destroyer HOBART shows. At least her sailors don't mind some spray in their considerably warmer weather. (Royal Australian Navy)

The landing ship SIR BEDIVERE was on passage from Norway to Dundee with Royal Marines vehicles on 29 February 1988 when this photograph was taken. The photographers diary for that day reads "Terribly rough...80 knots wind...120ft waves. Hove to until late afternoon." This photograph taken that morning came after a "worrying time" the previous night. The Satellite Navigation receiver fell off its mounting and loud crashing noises during the night revealed, the next morning, the top mast collapsed.
(Stuart Talton)

Whilst on deck only one Land Rover suffered any damage when it had its door wrenched off. Below decks several cracks developed in the forward collision bulkhead which delayed the vessel sailing again after reaching the calmer waters of Dundee Harbour. (Stuart Talton)

At their normal operating depths nuclear submarines such as TIRELESS, shown here, experience very little - if any - movement. “On the roof”, as the surface is known by submariners, its a different story as the round hull doesn't have bilge keels fitted to reduce rolling. (MoD/Crown Copyright)

Punching through the swell the frigate ANDROMEDA gives her upper deck a good covering of salt water. It will all have to be scrubbed off before her next arrival in port if she is to look her best. This photograph was taken in June 1989 in the North Atlantic as she approached APPLELEAF for fuel. (George Mortimore)

The Mediterranean was neither balmy or blue in May 1989 when this photograph was taken of the Danish Frigate NIELS JUEL. Just visible on her beam is her sister PETER TORDENSKIOLD. They are seen taking station on the tanker BLUE ROVER whose fuelling hose hangs ready to pass to the frigate when she is on station. (George Mortimore)

Built of Glass Reinforced Plastic with the majority of their hull out of the water and very little below these Hunt class minecountermeasure vessels are renowned to be "lively" in a seaway. Here ATHERSTONE is photographed in the English Channel. The Nab Tower can just be seen on the horizon. (MoD/Crown Copyright)

Snapped by the Officer of the Watch, from the relative comfort of the bridge, IRON DUKE takes on a huge wave in the North Atlantic. The ship was conducting Arctic Trials at about 70 degrees North, heading towards Bear Island. The wave height was around 40-50 feet. The photographer wryly noted that "at the time the sea was calming down after a Northerly storm force 10 during the previous night!" (Mark Mitchell)

Storm - Very high waves, long overhanging crests, tumbling heavy and shock-like foam in large patches blown in dense white streaks, surface of sea white in appearance; visibility affected. (Beaufort Wind Scale definition). (MoD/Crown Copyright)

Pictured in 1993 whilst part of the Standing Naval Force Atlantic (SNFL) the diminutive Norwegian frigate OSLO gamely tries to keep station with the larger members of the squadron as they head west across the Atlantic for the sunnier waters of the Caribbean. (Steve Bush)

Naval exercises in the North Atlantic often encounter rough weather. Teamwork 1993 was no exception. The American destroyer NICHOLSON tries to keep station astern of the tanker awaiting her turn for a top up of fuel. (Steve Bush)

Multiple ship replenishments can turn what appears to be quite a smooth sea into a boiling cauldron in very short order. Here the interaction between the Australian tanker SUCCESS and the frigates SYDNEY (03) and DARWIN (04) is very noticeable. (Royal Australian Navy)

The US tanker NEOSHO sits solidly in mid Atlantic during the same exercise valiantly dispensing much needed fuel to the escorts. The Canadian SKEENA on her starboard side is preparing to receive the hose from the forward RAS rig, whilst the hose streamed out from the port RAS station is attached (at the third attempt) to the Type 22 frigate BRAVE. The rolling motion of the ships meant that the hoses went from being stretched taut as here, to dragging in the sea on the opposite roll! (Steve Bush)

The Australian tanker WESTRALIA (the former RFA APPLELEAF) and the guided missile frigate ADELAIDE carry out a replenishment at sea in wintry conditions in the Indian Ocean - in 1997. The difficulties of this type of evolution are amply illustrated here as the two ships rise and fall out of synchronisation due to their different dimensions and the confused sea state created by their close proximity. (Royal Australian Navy)

The Danish Frigate TRITON crashing through northern waters during a search and rescue operation. (Maritime Photographic)

The Belgian Navy minehunter ASTER enthusiastically demonstrates the types reputation for "bouncy" rides. (Christian Louis)

The Royal Australian Navy frigate ANZAC punched through the icy Southern Ocean as she headed south to patrol in the Heard Island region for illegal fishermen during "Operation Dirk" - in November 1997. This is a good illustration of how the bow flare is designed to keep water away from the forecastle. (Royal Australian Navy)

Since 1982 LEEDS CASTLE (and her sister DUMBARTON CASTLE) have rotated duties as the Falkland Islands Patrol Vessel (FIPV). Here she approaches the Falkland Islands Guardship BRAVE in 1997 for a light jackstay transfer in typical cold and grey South Atlantic weather. Much to the relief of the forecastle party (hidden behind yet another wave) the evolution was cancelled shortly after this picture was taken! (Steve Bush)

The Canadian Patrol vessel EDMONTON is subjected to a bumpy ride whilst operating in the Pacific. (Dave Scoble Collection)

The Joint Maritime Courses held off the Scottish coast are always a good breeding ground for rough seas. Towards the end of 2000 the Type 23 frigate LANCASTER is seen battling through heavy seas. It is in conditions such as these that many NATO navies hone their skills in all areas of naval warfare. (Lt Cdr Talbot/Lt Ellis RN)

O Eternal Lord God, who alone spreadest out the heavens and rulest the raging of the sea; who hast encompassed the waters with bounds until day and night come to an end; be pleased to receive into thy Almighty and most gracious protection the persons of us thy servants, and the fleet in which we serve........

The Naval Prayer

Sailors always take comfort from the fact that after the storm comes the calm. The Dutch submarine DOLFIJN surfaces into a tranquil sea. (Steve Bush)

INDEX